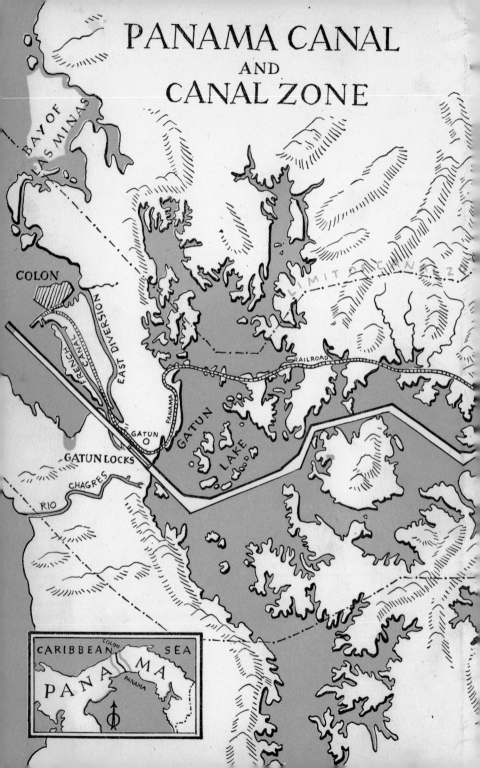

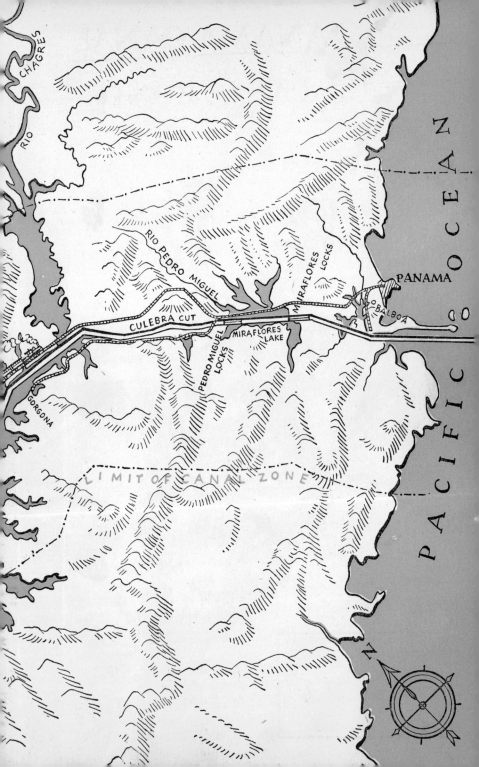

PANAMA CANAL

THE
PANAMA
CANAL

★

by **BOB CONSIDINE**

Illustrated by **FRITZ KREDEL**

Landmark
BOOKS

RANDOM HOUSE · NEW YORK

986.2
C765p

Copyright 1951 by Bob Considine

Published in New York by Random House, Inc.
and simultaneously in Toronto, Canada by
Random House of Canada Ltd.

Manufactured in the U. S. A.

CONTENTS

CHAPTER I

The Narrow Land

THE DREAM OF A WATERWAY THROUGH THAT
slender cord of mountain and jungle which
unites North and South America—the Isthmus
of Panama—first took shape in the mind of
Christopher Columbus.

3

For all his wishful thinking and prayerful hopes, Columbus knew by the end of his second trip to the New World that he was a failure. He knew that despite the support of Spain's Queen Isabella and King Ferdinand, he had not made good on his promise to open a new westerly route to the precious stores of the Indies.

It was on his third voyage, which brought him on August 1, 1498 to the shores of South America, that Columbus first learned from the natives of "a narrow land between two seas." But there was no opportunity to find it and seek what he hoped would be a waterway through it. The greed and cruelty of many of the adventurers he had left behind as colonizers after his first two trips had made enemies of the natives. The "narrow land" would have to wait until he could restore order.

But even order escaped him. There had been stirred up against him at home a great muttering by the disappointed colonists who had found their way back to Spain. They paraded before the palaces of the King and Queen, denouncing the explorer.

King Ferdinand, always lukewarm to Columbus, who was of lowly birth and not a Spaniard, dispatched Francisco Bobadilla to Hispaniola (now Haiti and the Dominican Republic). Columbus was returned in chains on a ship commanded by Alonso Vallejo, whom he had schooled.

Yet the heart of Isabella was touched once more, and on May 9, 1502, Columbus sailed on his fourth and last voyage. Ferdinand had stripped him of all remaining governing authority in the New World, but this caused only relief in the mind of the explorer. For now he would be free to press on to the "narrow land." He prayed that he might even find a way to travel beyond that, to the Indies he had been seeking so long.

Columbus had been ordered to stay away from Hispaniola. However, fate ruled that he not only touch there but be present at the undoing of Bobadilla, who had replaced him. With his ship in need of repairs, Columbus sought a haven against an approaching hurricane as he lay off Hispaniola. But Bobadilla, who was busy loading slaves, gold, and the fruits of the land aboard a fleet of galleons and caravels, coldly rejected the discoverer's plea. Let the timbers of Columbus's ship rot, and him with them, Bobadilla ruled. He laughed scornfully as Columbus' ship moved on to find shelter in the lee of the island. And he himself sailed, knowing that when he arrived in Spain with his great treasures, he would sit at the place in court reserved for the once mighty Admiral. But he and all who sailed with him were lost in the hurricane.

Saved by his seamanship, Columbus sailed

on. At Honduras he heard again not only of the "narrow land" but, as his heart leaped, of rich, gold-littered lands that lay beyond. There, at long last, must be the jeweled cities of Cathay and the Grand Khan himself.

Christopher Columbus found the Isthmus of Panama. Indeed, he debarked momentarily at what is now the city of Colon at the Atlantic mouth of the Panama Canal. There is reason to believe that in a longboat he ventured up the twisting Chagres River, Nature's unsuccessful attempt at a canal.

But apparently he saw nothing that made him sense that he was probing the connecting cord of the two great land masses of the New World at its slenderest point. Inland, his disappointed eyes beheld the dry, impenetrable barrier of the Continental Divide. He left Panama, never knowing that he was treading on land which would change the history of the world.

Thirteen years later, by which time Columbus was dust, a debt-ridden conquistador named Vasco Nunez de Balboa hurriedly left a New World suburb of Hispaniola. Concealed in a barrel of provisions, he ended up in Darien near the Gulf of Uraba in present-day Colombia.

In time Balboa rose to the command of the squalid little colony at Santa Maria de la Antigua del Darien. Meanwhile he had managed to gain the confidence of the Indian tribes of the region.

From the chieftain of one of these Balboa heard an extension of the story that had been told to Columbus. There was not only the "narrow land," Balboa was told, but a vast ocean that lay on the opposite side of the land beyond the inland mountain range. If one sailed down the endless coastline that touched the great sea he would come, at last, to a land rich in gold and precious man-made treasures (Peru).

Balboa's longing for the gold and man-made treasures was greater than his longing for a view of a new body of water. At once he made plans to find and invade the fabled land where the treasures could be found. But a ship that touched at the colony brought him word that his enemies had spoken against him in Spain, and he was ordered to return to face trial. He must have been a man of great charm and skilled in argument, for he won a brief reprieve. He would, he decided, do something quickly that would win back the King's friendship and give the lie to his accusers.

So on September 1, 1513, he began his march across the Isthmus with his friend Francisco Pizarro, the eventual conqueror of Peru, and about 1,500 others, mainly natives. It took Balboa twenty-five days to reach the top of the range on which Columbus's tired eyes had rested.

And from that elevation Vasco Nunez de

11

Balboa looked down on a quiet sea which, because the Isthmus twists and turns like an angry snake, lay to the south.

He called it the Great South Sea and claimed it and all the lands it touched for Spain. Then he dispatched Pizarro and two others toward the water, as scouts. Four days later Balboa himself arrived at the Pacific's side. There he quickly gathered up such souvenirs as were available and composed a glowing report in which he gave himself fulsome praise. The gifts and the announcement he sent back to his King, Ferdinand The Catholic.

The King was pleased enough to name Balboa "Admiral of the South Sea." But almost immediately Balboa's enemies went to work again. While he built ships and plotted the advance on Peru's riches he was imprisoned by his successor as Chief Magistrate of Santa Maria de la Antigua del Darien. This man was Pedrarias, who forced Balboa's conviction on a

12

charge of treason and had him put to death.

Pedrarias lived on to build a string of settlements across the narrow waist of what we now call Panama. And it was this murderously ambitious man, also known in history as Pedro Arias de Avila, who was the first European to confirm Columbus's doubts. He learned with certainty that no waterway cuts through that string of land on which he had built his settlements.

It was Pedrarias, too, who ordered built in 1519 the first crude road across the Isthmus, back-breakingly achieved by native labor. History does not record the cost of the road in lives, nor the names of the job's whip-waving section bosses. It does record, however, that this was the only road across the entire Isthmus for the next fifteen years. Part of its stone foundation, worn smooth by the bare feet of generations of Indians, may be seen to this day.

In 1529 Alvaro de Saavedra Ceron made

the first clear-cut proposal that a canal be dug through the Isthmus. He suggested the general area where the Panama Canal was later built.

Five years later Charles V ordered that a study be made of a canal's possibility. Such a canal was to use the Chagres on the Atlantic side and the San Juan River on the Pacific side. But the governor of the region informed Charles V that studies showed it to be an impossible task.

Philip II of Spain, who sent his ill-starred armada against England, also showed a lively but strange interest in the Isthmus. It was his desire to build there a canal through which loot from pillaged Peru could be carried to Spain. Poring over the report of a commission he had formed to lay out a canal, Philip decreed that no man ever would create such a waterway.

"God has shown his will," the monarch ruled. However, he wanted to make certain that he

14

would not be proven wrong, and also to protect the monopoly Spain held on Isthmian transportation. For these reasons, Philip further decreed that any man who attempted to build across the Isthmus a new passage of any type could be put to death.

The terrible pronouncement remained in effect for 200 years.

CHAPTER II

The Belt
of Steel

LATE IN THE 1700's, BARON ALEXANDER VON Humboldt, one of the great naturalists of history, set aside the rich honors he had won in his native Germany and set sail to join Napoleon Bonaparte in Egypt. Accompanied by his botanist companion, Aimé Bonpland, von Humboldt's ship touched at Spain, where he was so royally received by court scholars that his plans underwent great change. He remained in Spain for several years, and in 1799 was given the Spanish ship *Pizarro* and agreed to study the neglected natural resources of Spain's possessions in the New World.

Von Humboldt's findings in the next five years covered a breath-taking range of study, reaching from the discovery that meteor showers can be predicted in advance to the first known treatise on the fertilizing properties of guano. He explored the upper reaches of the Amazon and established its relationship to the Orinoco.

But he was especially absorbed by his pack trips back and forth across the Isthmus. After his return to Europe in 1804 he published a paper in which he carefully traced no less than nine possible routes for canals that would link the two great oceans. His sites reached from lower Mexico to a point just below the present Canal.

The accounts of his voyages were the best-sellers of the next twenty years. His comments on the possibility of a canal moved Goethe, the immortal German author, to write:

"This work will be done one day, but I shall not see it, just as I shall not live to see the Suez Canal. I should have liked to have lived several centuries later, in order to see these two gigantic undertakings completed."

Von Humboldt brought great learning back to Spain to deliver to the hands and minds of his patrons. But it was a gift to a sick nation which had neither the will nor the means to retain its colonies in the New World.

With one last effort, Spain in 1814 set up a company to build a canal at one of the nine suggested sites. But during the next ten years, the nation lost most of its holdings in the Americas.

At about this time a nation which the Spanish grandees could only consider an upstart, the United States of America, was beginning to take an interest in a canal across the Isthmus. Von Humboldt's writings had had wide reception in Congress, and from 1820 until the United States bought the Panama Canal Zone, no session of Congress was free of canal debate.

The young United States plainly resented the interest which Britain, Germany and France showed in building a canal. President James Monroe, in his classic message to the Congress on December 2, 1823, stated his country's case in broad but blunt terms:

"The American continents, by the free and independent condition which they have assumed and maintained, are henceforth not to be considered as subjects for future colonization by any European powers. . . . It is impossible for the European governments to interfere in their (South America's and Central America's) concerns without affecting us."

And as for the canal itself, Henry Clay proclaimed that if one were built it would be constructed by the United States alone, and that it would be "free to all nations on equal terms."

France paid no attention to these remarks from across the sea. Between the years 1825 and 1846, she sent a number of missions to the Isthmus to examine von Humboldt's sites as well as others. One French plan was to dig a canal across Nicaragua, because Lake Nicaragua covers about a third of the 150-mile distance between the oceans.

In 1838 France obtained a concession from the Republic of New Granada (now Colombia and Panama) to build a railway across the Isthmus at a point near the present canal. Five years later, the French engineer Napoleon Garella made the most careful survey up to that time. He informed his government that a canal could be built (near the present site), but passage would have to involve at least thirty-four locks. Garella explained that the Pacific was a higher body of water than the Atlantic.

France's railway rights on the Isthmus lapsed. It remained for a United States that was discovering and settling its western frontier to complete what France had failed to do.

The Congress, in 1848, gave its blessing to two United States steamship lines whose vessels reached down from New York and San Francisco like a huge pincers to clasp the Isthmus in the grip of American influence. At first it seemed a daring adventure, financially. The number of passengers and amount of cargo carried by the line from New York (and New Orleans) to the mouth of the Chagres River on the Atlantic side of the Isthmus was small at first, but adequate.

William H. Aspinwall's Pacific Mail Steamship Company, whose ships sailed down the Pacific from California (and later Oregon) to Panama City, had greater difficulty in making ends meet.

But if the ocean voyages to Panama were considered hard, the short trip across the Isthmus was a task that called for tough pioneers.

Passengers alighting at the end of the voyage to the Chagres descended shaky ladders and stumbled into rocking little rowboats. Braving the elements and the wildness of the sea, the small boats would then be driven to the beach. Sometimes passengers and their baggage were dumped into the surf.

Once on shore and dried off, the passengers were placed in longboats which natives laboriously poled up the Chagres River. Their trip on the Chagres depended entirely on the season. In the rainy season, when the river was as full as it

25

was rough, the travelers advanced as far as Las Cruces. In the dry season they could reach only to Gorgona. Overnight stops were in dirty, mosquito-buzzing huts.

At the end of this stage of the trip, the passengers were transferred to burros for the tortuous ascent and descent of the mountains. Then, if the Rio Grande was in a gentle mood, they climbed back into longboats and were poled the remainder of the way to the Pacific.

The average time of passage was a week, but for many it stretched into eternity. Road and river accidents took their toll. One had to chance death from poisonous snakes, and death or long illnesses from the rotten food, unclean drinking water, and mosquitos.

Far to the north, in the young United States, men laid plans for a railroad across the treacherous Isthmus. Their leader was John Lloyd Stephens, who knew the region as a travel-

writer. Aspinwall, financier Henry Chauncey and others raised the money needed.

It was not hard money to find, for an event of mighty importance had occurred in California. Gold had been discovered, and the rich yellow metal was drawing people westward like a great magnet. From the eastern part of the country, California could be reached only by long and hard travel across the plains and over the mountains. The golden spike that was to link a tight band of railroad track across the United States would not be driven for another generation.

So the Forty-Niners had to risk death in dangerous cross-country travel by covered wagon or death or disease on the trip over the Isthmus by longboat and burro. A third route was possible. They might sail around the southern tip of South America. Plainly, a railroad across the Isthmus must be built.

The Panama Railroad came into existence as a corporation on April 7, 1849, with a stock value of $1,000,000. The United States Government showed a keen interest by assigning some of its best Army engineers to the task of laying the rails. One of these, Colonel George M. Totten, was in charge of the early portion of the historic work, with the distinguished civil engineer John C. Trautwine as his chief aide.

That it was to be an undertaking filled with great difficulties soon became apparent to Totten, Trautwine, and the other pioneers. It was their early plan to lay the railroad from the Pacific side of the Isthmus. The first section of the tracks would cover that portion of the trip (twenty miles) then attended to by burros. But in the path of the intended railroad lay the mountains. Even though the engineers knew of the 300-foot pass called Culebra across the mountains, the task seemed too difficult for human skill.

After a costly delay of nearly half a year, Totten, Trautwine, and the others altered their plans and commenced the work on the Atlantic side. Work crews labored with their heads and hands encased in suffocating gauze as a defense against the insects. Living conditions among the lower-class workers corresponded roughly to those which must have existed among the slaves and captives who built the pyramids of ancient Egypt.

In distant New York, stockholders demanded greater and greater efforts, for they saw in a completed railroad a gold mine greater than any California possessed. But after two years of back-breaking labor, only eight miles of track had been laid.

By July 16, 1852, about half of the fifty-mile line was completed. Events of that day, and of subsequent days, will help the reader understand the difficulties of Isthmian travel.

Late on July 16 the United States mail steamer *Ohio* arrived at the town of Aspinwall, since re-named Colon in honor of Christopher Columbus. ("Colon" is the Spanish version of the name "Columbus.") Aboard the Ohio were eight companies of the Fourth Infantry of the United States. With their families they numbered 700 people. They were the first United

States troops and the first Army wives and children to cross the Isthmus and head for duty on the distant shore of California. They were quartermastered by a captain named Ulysses S. Grant, who later became commanding general of the Union armies of the Civil War and President of the United States. It was Grant's job to move the group to a waiting vessel on the Pacific side.

One of his first concerns was the cholera epidemic then raging in Aspinwall. Then it was found that the gear the Army had brought along for use in California was too heavy for the feeble locomotives of the Panama Railroad to pull. The trip to the end of the line had to be made in relays, while the danger of sickness spread. Some of the officers and men and their families boarded trains to Gorgona, where the women and children took burros. The men marched on foot to the seas.

But when Captain Grant and his group arrived at Cruces, all the animals assigned to them as beasts of burden had been rented for higher prices by frantic Forty-Niners eager to get on to the Pacific. It took Grant's group, and some of the earlier units which marched to the sea, four weeks to cross the Isthmus even though the railroad covered half of the fifty-mile distance. By the time the forlorn troops and their kin reached California, more than 150 of their number had perished. Captain Grant took the brunt of the blame for the disaster. The *Panama Herald* said of him:

"Unfitted by either natural ability or education for the post he occupied, he evinced his incapacity at every moment."

But an event of even more importance and (later) of greater embarrassment was brewing. The British did not like the idea of an American-controlled railroad across the Isthmus. Nor did members of the British Parliament who were unfriendly to the United States ac-

cept the growing understanding in America that if a canal ever were built across the Isthmus, the United States would build it.

On New Year's Day, 1849, the British made a "show of might." A man o' war flying the Union Jack appeared off San Juan de Nicaragua, course of the proposed alternate route across the Isthmus, and took possession of the settlement.

The United States felt itself in no position to

question this violation of its Monroe Doctrine.
It appeased England with a treaty, signed in
1850 and known as the Clayton-Bulwer Treaty.
By its terms, Britain was to have equal rights
and duties in the development of an Isthmian
canal either at Panama or Nicaragua. Both
Britain and the United States pledged that the
canal area would be arranged by pact with the
country concerned and that the area would not
be fortified. They also agreed that in the event
of war the zone would be held neutral and left
open to the shipping of the two powers.

In exchange for these concessions, Britain
agreed not to interfere in any way with the
building of the American railroad across Panama. The promoters and engineers of this undertaking were greatly relieved. They were already having more than their just share of troubles. John L. Stephens, whose dream the railroad had been in the first place and who had
worked wonders there under cruel circum-

stances, died—probably of yellow fever. In addition, a portion of the bridge which the engineers had built across the Chagres at Barbacoas after painful labor and great expense, splintered like matchwood during a flood of the river.

Horrible tales reached the United States about the death rate among the railroad workers. It was said that there was a death for every tie laid. But this was not quite true—though deaths from all causes were hardly light. More than 800 men gave their lives to this work, out of a total work force of about 6,000. The victims had come from the ends of the earth—from England and Ireland, Germany and France, China and India, from the Caribbean islands and from Central and South America.

Deaths were greatest among the Chinese (about 400). Many of the Chinese either bought or were supplied with opium, to make them forget the hardships of jungle and mountain grade. The Chinese produced the greatest number of suicides.

On the other hand, the Americans produced the greatest number of hoodlums and highwaymen, who made a comfortable living raiding the growing railroad and its worker-settlements. Law enforcement was in the weak hands of New Granada (Colombian) police and soldiers, many of whom were in secret partnership with the bandits. It was not until an adventuring former Texas Ranger named Ran Runnels formed a "shoot-first-and-ask-questions-later" posse that the murderous robber bands were run from the Isthmus.

Despite all the difficulties that faced the railroad builders, work went on surely. In a driving rain at midnight, January 27, 1855, the rails were finally joined. This took place at a point thirty-seven miles from Aspinwall and ten and a half miles from Panama City. The mighty Atlantic and Pacific Oceans had, at long last, been joined by steel rails through American skill and drive. The job had taken five years and cost $8,000,000. It altered the economy of that part of the world and its very way of life. And it was a time for chest-swelling in the United States.

CHAPTER III

Ferdinand de Lesseps

Nearly ten years before the first work was
started on the Panama Railroad by the American company, a French group had been formed
to build just such a railway. It had won a concession from New Granada which was similar
to the one the Americans eventually held. Be-

41

cause the French company lacked money, it let its rights lapse.

Now with the completion of the railroad by the United States, France became determined to build a Panama Canal as soon as its great task of building the Suez Canal was finished.

By 1870, France regarded the building of the Panama Canal as a national duty. The country had been defeated in a war with Germany and it was eager to prove to the world that France was still a major power. This could be done by completing a great and difficult engineering feat.

France was aided in its ambition by a running diplomatic battle then being fought between the United States and Great Britain. The people of the United States, especially those in the victorious Northern states after the Civil War, would no longer accept the Clayton-Bulwer Treaty of 1850.

We set out to break that treaty by the terms of which England was to be an equal partner in the building and control of a canal when and if a canal were built.

In 1867 Secretary of State Hamilton Fish wrote to our minister in Bogota, "The President [Andrew Johnson] regards it [the canal] as an American enterprise, which he desires to be carried out under American auspices, to the benefit of which the whole commercial world should be fully admitted."

Ten years later President Rutherford B. Hayes, in a special message to Congress, said, "The policy of this country is a canal under American control: the United States cannot consent to the surrender of this control to any European country."

The "European country" foremost in the minds of Americans was England. The United States speeded up its surveys of possible canal routes from lower Mexico to the area of the Panama Railroad, and hammered away at England for a revision of the Treaty.

In 1876 President Grant, a Canal champion who could speak with some authority, tried without success to make an acceptable 99-year treaty with Colombia (Panama was then a province of Colombia). As a result, the interest of the United States swung toward a Nicaraguan canal.

While we wrangled and attempted to make up our minds, the French moved. Not even the United States could deny France's preeminence in the field, for the whole world still thrilled to the creation of the Suez Canal.

And no one questioned that in Ferdinand de Lesseps, diplomat turned engineer, France possessed a genius who was best fitted to join the oceans by waterway. The "Great Frenchman," as he was known, was honored throughout the world, and rightly so. Had he not recently com-

44

pleted at Suez an engineering feat which man had first attempted as far back as a thousand years before Christ?

In 1871 the International Geographical Congress, French-dominated, met at Antwerp and listened attentively to a report from Anthoine de Gogorza. This man was an American-born French explorer who had traveled extensively through Colombia's province of Panama.

De Gogorza's description of possible canal routes through Panama aroused great interest in France. Many French people who had been small stockholders in the Suez Canal were looking for new fields, and canals, in which to invest their earnings.

The great de Lesseps came more clearly into the picture in 1875. In a speech before the Geographical Society of Paris, he pictured a profitable sea-level ditch that could be built through the Isthmus of Panama.

Matters moved swiftly after that. An organization named the French Committee for Cutting the Interoceanic Canal, with de Lesseps as president, was formed. It commissioned de Gogorza to return to Colombia and secure from that country an agreement permitting the French to dig.

The Colombian Government, which at that time seemed ready to sign any agreement if a promise of large enough payments was made, quickly agreed.

But it was apparent even to the greatest dreamers among the French that they must learn considerably more about the Panama Isthmus. On November 6, 1876, the Committee dispatched a group of engineers to Panama aboard the steamer *Lafayette*.

Chief engineer of the group was French Naval Lieutenant Lucien N. B. Wyse, a descendent of the Bonapartes and well connected, socially and financially, in France.

When Wyse returned to France the following

year, he reported that Colombia would be more easily dealt with than Nicaragua, for Nicaragua was then entertaining offers from the Americans. Wyse also believed that any canal across the Panama Isthmus would entail the building of locks, because of the differences in Atlantic and Pacific tides and the difference in sea levels of the two oceans.

De Lesseps, a figure of imposing authority and occasional arrogance, laughed at the statement that locks must be built and sent Wyse back to Panama for further studies and negotiations.

This time Wyse chose the exact strip of land through which the canal eventually was dug. (He conceded that a 7,720 meter tunnel through Culebra might make possible a lockless passage between the oceans.) Wyse then went on to Bogota by horseback and made a binding agreement with Colombia (March 20, 1878) to begin work on the canal.

Wyse discovered while in Bogota that France would probably have to buy the American-owned Panama Railroad because of certain rights earlier sold and given to that line. So Wyse journeyed to New York and gained an option to buy the road. He was welcomed by the company executives, whose profits had been growing smaller since the opening of the transcontinental railway across the United States.

On Wyse's return to Paris a confident de Lesseps called an International Congress for Consideration of an Interoceanic Canal. Among the 138 delegates were eleven Americans, but they took little part in the proceedings. United States' interest in an Isthmian canal was by now devoted almost exclusively to Nicaragua, and a national depression had dulled even that. An economy wave in the Federal government had caused the nation to close many of its diplomatic and consular offices through Central and South America.

De Lesseps was the leading figure at the assembly. He overrode all opposition to a sea-level route by the immense weight of his reputation. He would not hear the protests of, among others, a French engineer named Adolphe Godin de Lepinay.

De Lepinay argued shrewdly that the available machinery of the day could not cut deeply enough through the mountains to permit the waters of the Atlantic and Pacific to be joined directly.

He suggested the creation of two large lakes on either side of the mountain. These were to be built by damming the Chagres on the Atlantic side and the Rio Grande on the Pacific.

Let the waters, he said, rise to about eighty feet, thus reducing the depth of the cut-through that would join them; then build lifting and lowering locks reaching out from the combined lakes to the oceans.

Many years later, after fortunes had been

lost and reputations ruined, United States engineers did precisely that.

But at the time of the proposal, de Lepinay's words were drowned out by de Lesseps and the others who believed that he could indeed build his water-level route if his heart was set on it. Of the seventy-eight "Yes" votes that decided in favor of the sea-level canal, only twenty were cast by engineers—and only one of those who voted "Yes" had ever seen Panama.

With de Lesseps as president, the ill-starred Panama Canal Company was formed. In its first announcement it stated that it would soon embark on a project which would cost 1,070,000,000 francs ($214,000,000 at that time). The announcement promised that the job would be completed in twelve years—unless new earth-moving equipment that could make the work go faster was developed in the meanwhile.

De Lesseps was seventy-four years old, but praise of both self-seekers and truly devoted followers overrode the advice of those closest to him. His faithful son, Charles, a fine engineer, pleaded:

"What do you wish to find at Panama? Money? You will not bother any more about money at Panama than you did at Suez. Is it glory? You have had enough glory. Why not leave that to someone else? And as for those of us who have worked at your side, are we to have no repose? The task of Panama is certainly grandiose, and I believe that it can be carried through, but think of the risk that will be run by those who put themselves at its head. You succeeded at Suez by a miracle. Be content with accomplishing one miracle in your lifetime, and do not hope for a second." *

When the father buoyantly replied that he felt like a general who, having won one great battle desires only to win a greater one, Charles shrugged and answered:

* *Suez and Panama* (Siegfried).

"Father, should you wish me to join you, I shall do so with the best will in the world. I shall not complain no matter what happens. All that I am I owe to you. What you have given me you have the right to take away."

The first of the countless bills that de Lesseps' company was to receive during its history was one for 10,000,000 francs. This money had been promised to Wyse and several of his associates for the agreements that Wyse had obtained from Colombia and the Panama Railroad.

The Panama Canal Company's first drive for funds, on August 6 and 7, 1879, sought 400,000,000 francs. It raised only 30,000,000.

This was an omen. From then until the dreary end the financing of France's dream of a canal was a vast promotion stunt. It created scandals which shook the nation's confidence in its cabinets and brought financial loss to hundreds of thousands of French investors.

One early difficulty was the grasping, money-

loving French press. French editors and newspaper owners demanded bribes to support the
fund-raising, and, when these demands were
not met satisfactorily, turned on the company
and denounced it as a fraud. French politicians
blackmailed the organization.

In dealing with these people, de Lesseps
proved to be a man of boundless energy and
imagination. To combat the unfriendly press he
started his own newspaper, *The Bulletin of the
Interoceanic Canal*, which appeared every
second week. Nearly every story told of the enormous profits which shareholders would one day
receive from traffic tolls paid by canal shipping.

Then the elderly man went "on the road."
Like a French Johnny Appleseed he spread the
gospel of the canal through every village of his
country. He was like a man running for office,
but one who sought funds rather than position.

When the bitter French press reminded pro-
spective investors that Panama was a "land of

pestilence and disease," de Lesseps replied by taking his wife and three of his younger children to the Isthmus. From there he sent to the *Bulletin* glowing accounts of the beauty of Panama and its healthful climate.

In February and March, 1880, he visited San Francisco, Chicago, Boston, New York and

Washington, and was welcomed everywhere. But the men he wished most to attract—American financiers—avoided him. President Hayes had boomed forth his message to the Congress, bluntly pledging an American-built canal under American control.

Not the least bit abashed, openly at least, de Lesseps cabled to his paper, "The message of the President has assured the security of the canal."

Then he returned home by way of England, Belgium and Holland, paid the necessary bribes to the French press, staged grand banquets and celebrations for himself, and managed to raise an additional 600,000,000 francs.

But if the Panama Canal Company's finances strengthened, its woes doubled and trebled.

The first French engineering teams sent to Panama encountered enormous difficulties. Some of its more valued men died there of yellow fever.

Another trouble arose when the American officials of the Panama Railroad demanded that the Colombian Government declare the French contract invalid. This demand was made because de Lesseps had not exercised the company's option to buy the road. The French company therefore had to buy the outdated railway at a cost of 100,000,000 francs. This was far above its true value.

After two costly years of surveying, and some trial digging, de Lesseps and his engineers agreed that the sea-level canal was to have a depth of twenty-nine and a half feet. It would be seventy-two feet wide at the bottom. This, they believed, would involve the moving of 157,-000,000 cubic yards of earth. The canal would connect Colon on the Atlantic side and Panama City on the Pacific side.

Several French contractors gave up in despair as mounting difficulties removed all their hope of profit through the early 1880s. Not the least of their problems was labor. The Indians of the region had been depended upon to produce the bulk of the canal-digging manpower. But they showed little interest in working at such a task, because kindly Nature provided them with their simple wants. The Chinese who were imported, along with opium rations, often quit to set up small businesses along the proposed route of the ditch. The bulk of the work was done eventually by men from Jamaica.

There was little thought of white labor. By the middle 1880s all of Western Europe and the United States knew of the very high death rate among white workers in Panama. De Lesseps was not permitted to forget the statements he had made earlier concerning the healthfulness of the land.

The wife, son, daughter (and daughter's fiancé) of Director General Jules Dingler died in a single month. Of twenty-four nuns and novices

who went to Panama from France to administer to the sick, twenty-one died.

But the French continued bravely in the face of killers which were not to be identified for another twenty years. These were the *anopheles* mosquito, carrier of malaria; and the *stegomyia* mosquito, carrier of yellow fever.

Nature defied the courageous men. The innocent-looking Chagres, which was at first considered a God-made river-way into the interior, and one which would save much digging, became a raging torrent with every cloudburst—and there were countless cloudbursts.

And, always facing the adventurers, there was the problem of digging an eight-mile trench (300 feet deep and seventy-three feet wide across the bottom) through the mountains at Culebra. More than a mile of that trench would have to be dug through the main height of the range.

Yet the French might have achieved it if the earth and the supposedly solid rock had not been subject to vast landslides. In a minute's time these often destroyed the backbreaking work of months.

De Lesseps' earliest private estimate was that the entire canal could be built by moving only 54,000,000 cubic meters of earth. His engineers later raised this estimate to 75,000,000, then to 120,000,000.

But to cut through Culebra alone, as the

59

Americans later proved, necessitated the moving of 116,000,000 cubic meters. Of this, 56,-000,000 cubic meters, more than de Lesseps' first estimate of the entire canal job were the result of landslides!

While the French company gnawed away at Culebra, wild charges of theft, extravagance, and waste were hurled against it in France. De Lesseps attempted to silence his critics with cash, and great sums were poured into that bottomless pit. But no amount of money was capable of silencing a bitterly anti-canal newspaper, *The Panama*. The word "Panamiste" became a crowning insult in the French language.

Funds became desperately low, but the hopeful old man—who still believed a lockless canal was possible—would not be dismayed.

In 1886 de Lesseps wrung from French politicians a promise to enact a law permitting a fund-raising lottery to be held. And then, at the age of eighty-one, he made a last great effort to transplant his own high hopes and zeal into the hearts of the workers on the scene.

He journeyed back to Panama and one day, while thousands cheered, he galloped his horse up to the peak of Culebra, his flowing robes fluttering like a proud flag.

But at home were endless delays over the passage of the lottery law. De Lesseps did not sit and fret. He went back on the road, telling the French of the progress he had seen in Panama, and through a touching appeal raised another 300,000,000 francs.

By the late Summer of 1887 most of that was gone, too. Tearfully the old man yielded to his engineers, who persuaded him that if he persisted in his attempt to build a sea-level canal it would mean financial disaster. A canal with locks would be more practical, they advised.

Another half a billion francs, at least, would

be needed for a canal with locks, all agreed. But de Lesseps and his friends had raised all the funds they could. Only a national lottery would save the remnants of their hopes for a canal.

They increased their pressure on the French deputies, pointing out that perhaps 400,000 French voters held a financial interest in the canal. If there were no lottery law enacted, de Lesseps' friends argued, those voters would blame the deputies and perhaps take measures against them at the next elections. The frightened Chamber passed the law.

But the lottery was a financial failure. From the start it was condemned by insufficiently bribed newspapers and by its opponents in the Chamber. At the height of the share-selling a report was spread through France that de Lesseps had died.

The failure had to be faced squarely. There just was not enough money even to start work on a lock canal.

De Lesseps threw himself upon the mercy of the Chamber, pleading that the French Government carry on the work as a matter of national pride. When that plea fell on deaf ears he asked that the Chamber approve the formation of a new private company which he hoped to form to salvage the old.

But the Chamber voted down the proposal, 256 to 181.

When the crushing word reached de Lesseps the old man wept, a handkerchief over his face to muffle the sound.

"This is impossible! This is horrible!" he cried. "I did not believe the French Chamber would sacrifice the interests of the nation. They forget the milliard and a half (billion and a half) of the savings of the French people that are compromised by this vote, and they could have saved all this by a firm decision. This will be a triumph for our enemies, and a disaster to our flag."

63

The word spread quickly that the end was near, and hundreds of weeping or angry investors marched on the company offices.

The defeated old man strode courageously through the mob, chin in the air, and mounting a platform cried out, "My friends! Your subscriptions are safe. Our adversaries are confounded, and we now have no need of financiers. You have saved yourself by your own exertions. The canal will be made!"

They believed him. In the great emotional scene that followed, with de Lesseps weeping with many others, deeply touched investors offered him more money—including the small savings of their children.

All through France men who respected de Lesseps tried to whip up new interest in the canal. The United States was blamed for its real and imagined role in the failure, especially the indifference of its bankers.

In Panama, men continued to work with

what they had at hand, but lay-offs soon devel-
oped. On May 15, 1889, all work was stopped.

Dredges and other earth-moving equipment
were left where they last were used. Tons of
other equipment were dropped, to rust or to
be hidden by the oncoming jungle. Bustling
little villages along the ditch became ghost
towns.

And the unconquered Culebra looked down on the wreckage. The small wound in its peak was still 240 feet above sea level.

In Paris, the wheels of justice, oiled by the disgruntled, sought to grind out proper punishment. Baron de Reinach, an early associate of Wyse and Turr, committed suicide. De Lesseps and his brilliant son, who had begged him to rest on his Suez laurels and then had worked loyally for the canal, were indicted for corruption.

At his trial Charles de Lesseps told the court that one French politician alone had demanded and received 375,000 francs in bribes from the company.

"But you could have called the police," the court chided.

Charles de Lesseps shrugged. "But what happens if the policeman himself is the person holding you up for ransom?"

It summed up the enormous scope of the bribes which had helped wreck the French effort.

Charles and his father were sentenced to five years in prison. But old Ferdinand knew little or nothing of his indictment, his trial (which he had been too ill to attend) and his sentence. Like his son, he was not obliged to serve the time.

Something had snapped in the old man's mind before the trials began. His waking hours were little more than extensions of his sleep. And on December 7, 1894, death ended his struggle.

Though work had officially stopped on the canal in 1889 the company kept a few employees in Panama for another ten years, to prove legally to Colombia that work was "continuing."

Eventually, the company felt, it would find a

buyer for its equipment, its work, and its lease on the canal area.

The company's patience was at last rewarded. The Spanish-American War had thrust the United States into the position of an empire. It now held possessions as separated as the Philippines and Puerto Rico.

But the war had also exposed the country's helplessness in the matter of quick communication lines. The United States Navy had been forced to send the cruiser *Oregon* from San Francisco to Cuba by way of the Horn, and it had taken three months.

The exhausted French company and its restless stockholders knew that it was now simply a matter of time before the books could be closed on the French effort—a lofty dream that had ended in despair.

CHAPTER IV

America Tackles
the Job

THE FIRST ATTEMPTS OF THE FRENCH TO SELL THE
United States their interests in the canal were
met with defeat.

Public and engineering sentiment in America
favored a Nicaraguan canal, and the United
States Government still held a long-standing

canal treaty with that country. In addition there was considerable bad feeling toward the French, whose forlorn and ill-starred effort was considered by many in the United States as a threat to the Monroe Doctrine.

The French first set a price of $109,141,500 on their holdings in Panama. This price included the digging and shoring up that had been done. But the French were in no position to enforce the set price, for the only customer in the world—the United States—had great sales resistance.

This Government's offer of $40,000,000 for the French rights in Panama struck the stockholders in the French company with dismay. The anger of the stockholders served only to arouse the United States to greater interest in the Nicaraguan route. Meanwhile, Congress prepared a bill that would appropriate $180,000,000 for the building of a canal through Nicaragua.

The French hastily accepted the $40,000,000 offer for its rights in Panama, believing that it was better than no offer at all. Almost immediately the United States changed its mind about Nicaragua and set up, in 1899, the Isthmian Canal Commission.

Another factor in America's change of heart was a completely false rumor that the disastrous eruption of Mt. Pelée, on the Island of Martinique, made construction of a Nicaraguan canal foolhardy! People forgot that Mt. Pelée and Nicaragua are 1,500 miles apart.

Now there was the unpopular Clayton-Bulwer Treaty of 1850 to get rid of. The United States, which was most definitely feeling its new-found muscles, saw no reason why England should have equal rights in the construction and control of the Panama passage.

England proved surprisingly agreeable to a treaty change for it was warring in South Africa with the Boers. As a result it welcomed

73

a release from its promise to provide funds and manpower for the difficult job of creating a canal.

The Hay-Pauncefote Treaty, which replaced the Clayton-Bulwer pact on November 18, 1901, gave the United States all rights to deal independently for a canal. It also approved America's right to close the canal in time of war, if it so chose, to British shipping. In exchange, the United States promised to open its canal to the shipping of all nations in time of peace, and to charge equal fees for passage through the canal.

When the time came in 1902 to make the final arrangements concerning the canal, President William McKinley was dead by an assassin's hand, and blunt, brilliant Theodore Roosevelt had become the youngest President in our history.

Now a new difficulty appeared. A clause in the contract between the French company and the Government of Colombia had given Colombia the right to approve or disapprove the entrance of a third party into the picture.

Roosevelt's Secretary of State, John Hay, therefore called upon Colombia to send representatives to Washington to confer with him. His request, which was considered in some Colombian and United States circles as more of an order than a suggestion, produced Martinez Silva.

Silva was quickly replaced by another representative, and that representative in turn was dislodged by his government as unfitted for the job. Finally a secretary of the Colombian Legation in Washington, named Herran, became his country's spokesman. It was he who signed the Hay-Herran Treaty on January 22, 1903.

The treaty gave to the United States a strip of land six miles wide over the general route laid out by de Lesseps' engineers, and gave the United States the right to police the zone and administer it. Colombia was to be paid $10,000,000 and, after nine years of operation of the canal, a yearly fee of $250,000. The United States ratified, or approved, it on March 17, 1903.

To the complete astonishment of the United States, the Colombian Congress showed some dislike of the treaty during the first moments of the would-be ratification session. Delegates denounced Herran and called for a complete revision of the treaty terms. They demanded $15,000,000 from the United States and $10,000,000 from the French. And they rejected all portions of the treaty dealing with the establishment of American courts of law in the proposed zone.

President Theodore Roosevelt thundered his annoyance and impatience with these demands. Secretary of State Hay joined him in calling them ridiculous.

But the Colombian Congress would not be

forced into approving a treaty it thought unjust. It believed that the United States had acted disgracefully and it saw, too, a chance to take over all the completed work and equipment of the French company at the expiration of the Colombian-French agreement. Some Colombian leaders believed that if their country had enough patience it would receive not only the $10,000,000 offered by the United States but also the $40,000,000 which the United States was prepared to pay France.

But the Colombians did not count on the great drive and determination of Theodore Roosevelt. Even more important, they placed too much faith in the loyalty of that section of Colombia which has become the Republic of Panama.

Panamanians twice had seceded from Colombia, first in 1841 and again in 1853. The arrival of the French and their money caused a vast wave of graft and dishonesty in the prov-

77

ince of Panama. In the hope of keeping as much money as possible in the area itself, and to keep political leaders in the distant capital of Bogota from getting any of it, Panamanians often formed revolutionary groups. These were quickly put down by Colombian troops and police.

The decision of the Colombian Congress to reject the United States offer brought sharp cries of anger from Panama. On November 3, 1903, a month after the Colombian Congress adjourned without accepting the Hay-Herran Treaty, independence again was declared in Panama City and the final revolution began.

Historians agree that if the United States did not directly stir up the revolution it at least played a leading role. Details of the uprising were discussed openly in Washington a full month before the first shot was fired. Money with which to pay the revolutionary troops was raised in New York and Washington. When

Bogota sent 500 troops to Colon by sea to put down the revolution, the troops were met by the United States Navy cruiser *Nashville*. The captain of the *Nashville* explained that he was there to invoke a United States-New Granada (Colombia) Treaty signed in 1846 guaranteeing the United States all rights to free passage across the Isthmus.

Eyebrows in world capitals went up another notch when the United States welcomed a Panama diplomatic representative in Washington while the revolution was still under way. He was Philippe Bunau-Varilla, actually one of the promoters of the French company and a passionate champion of a Panama canal.

Though not a Panamanian (he was a French citizen) Bunau-Varilla was hailed in Washington. Quickly he signed the treaty which made possible the United States canal effort. It is the Hay-Bunau-Varilla Treaty. Representatives of Panama's new government who arrived in Washington several days after Bunau-Varilla were unhappy to learn that they had journeyed in vain. The pact had been sealed in their name by one whom they regarded as a foreign promoter.

The Hay-Bunau-Varilla Treaty was almost a carbon copy of the Hay-Herran Treaty, with Panama's name replacing Colombia's. The same financial terms were prescribed: an outright payment of $10,000,000 and $250,000 a year after the canal's ninth year of operation. It called, however, for a ten-mile corridor through Panama, instead of the original six-mile strip. Under the new treaty, there was to be greater control of the area by United States authorities than was originally asked of Colombia.

Theodore Roosevelt knew that he was being criticized abroad. During the course of the canal's construction he wrote what was, for him, almost an apology. It appeared in *The Outlook*.

The following paragraphs taken from it, throw light on his manner of reasoning. They also show a boldness of purpose that was to disappear, for better or worse, from our diplomacy:

"No other great work now being carried on throughout the world is of such far-reaching and lasting importance as the Panama Canal. Never before has a work of this kind on so colossal a scale been attempted. . . .

" . . . It must be a matter of pride to every honest American, proud of the good name of his country, that the acquisition of the Canal and the building of the Canal, in all their details, were as free from scandal as the public acts of George Washington and Abraham Lincoln.

Of course there was at the time (the acquisition) much repetition of state-

81

ments that I acted in an 'unconstitu-
tional' manner, that I 'usurped authority' which was not mine. The simple
fact was that when the interest of the
American people imperatively demanded that a certain act should be
done, and I had the power to do it, I
did it unless it was specifically pro-
hibited by law, instead of timidly re-
fusing to do it unless I could find some
provision of law which rendered it im-
perative that I should do it.

"In other words, I gave the benefit
of the doubt to the people of the
United States, and not to any group of
bandits, foreign or domestic, whose
interests happened to be adverse to
those of the people of the United
States. In my judgment, history had
taught the lesson that the President
has very great powers if he chooses to

exercise those powers; but that, if he is a timid or selfish man, afraid of responsibility and afraid of risks, he can of course manufacture ingenious excuses for failure to exercise them.

"In October and November, 1903, (the revolution in Panama) events occurred on the Isthmus of Panama which enabled me, and which made it my highest duty to the people of the United States, to carry out the provisions of the law of Congress. I did carry them out, and the Canal is now being built because of what I thus did. It is also perfectly true that, if I had wished to shirk my responsibility, if I had been afraid of doing my duty, I could have pursued a course which would have been technically defensible, which would have prevented criticism of the kind that has been made,

85

and which would have left the United States no nearer building the Canal at this moment than it had been for the preceding half-century.

"I would have taken the action I actually did take even though I had been certain that to do so meant my prompt retirement from public life at the next election; for the only thing that makes it worthwhile to hold a big office is taking advantage of the opportunities the office offers to do some big thing that ought to be done and is worth doing.

" . . . We negotiated with the representatives of Colombia a treaty which granted to Colombia even greater advantages than were subsequently granted to the Republic of Panama, a treaty so good that after

86

it had been rejected by Colombia, and after we had recognized Panama, Colombia clamored for leave to undo the past and enter into the treaty. But the Colombian Government, for reasons which, I regret to say, were apparently very bad indeed, declined to consummate the treaty to which their representatives had agreed.

"The Isthmus was seething with revolutionary spirit. The central government of the Republic of Colombia was inefficient and corrupt. Lawlessness had long been dominant in every branch. During a period of something like seventy years there had been only one or two instances in which a President had served out his term. . . .

87

"There was no need for any outsider to excite revolution in Panama. It was not a case of lighting a fuse that would fire a mine—there were dozens of such fuses being lit all the time; it was simply a case of its ceasing to be the duty of the United States to stamp on these fuses, or longer to act in the interest of those who had become the open and malignant foes of the United States—and of civilization and of the world at large.

" . . . Be it remembered that unless I had acted exactly as I did act there would now be no Panama Canal. . . . Every man who at any stage has opposed or condemned the action actually taken in acquiring the right to dig the Canal has really been the opponent of any and every effort that could ever have been made to dig the Canal. . . .

"The United States has done very much more than its duty to Colombia. Although Colombia had not the slightest claim to consideration of any kind, yet, in the interests of Panama and Colombia, the United States some time ago agreed to a tri-party treaty between herself, Colombia, and Panama, by which, as a simple matter of grace and not of right, adequate and generous compensation would have been given Colombia for whatever damage she had suffered; but Colombia refused to agree to the treaty. . . . There is no more reason for giving Colombia money to soothe her feelings for the loss of what she forfeited by her misconduct in Panama in 1903 than for giving Great Britain money for what she lost in 1776. . . .

"Not only was the course followed as regards Panama right in every detail and at every point, but there could have been no variation from this course except for the worse. We not only did what was demanded by every ethical consideration, national and international. We did our duty by the world, we did our duty by the people of Panama, we did our duty by ourselves. We did harm to no one save as harm is done to a bandit by a policeman who deprives him of his chance for blackmail. The United States has many honorable chapters in its history, but no more honorable chapter than that which tells of the way in which our right to dig the Panama Canal was secured. . . ."

Years later, during the administration of President Warren Harding, the United States presented to Colombia not only its regrets for past injustices but also the sum of $25,000,000.

CHAPTER V

Wallace, Stevens, and Gorgas

THE AMERICANS WHO BELIEVED THAT THE HACK-
ing out of a canal across Panama would be a
simple task, easily solved by American clever-
ness and drive, had many disappointments in
store for them.

The seven-man Isthmian Canal Commission

appointed by President Theodore Roosevelt sailed for Panama in April, 1904, and while there on a brief inspection tour made a costly decision. In effect they rejected the French belief that any canal cut through the Isthmus would have to contain locks.

As chief engineer for the enormous project they selected John F. Wallace, former president of the American Society of Civil Engineers, who had come up through the railroading ranks to gain his fine reputation. He accepted the $25,000-a-year job reluctantly, fearing that he would be bossed by all seven members of the Commission, few of whom had engineering training.

Wallace had other misgivings. After he and Mrs. Wallace had arrived in the Canal Zone it became known there and back in the States that he had brought along two metal coffins for use if he and his wife died of the diseases of the land.

His first task was a huge house-cleaning job. It was expected of him to use much of the equipment left behind by the French. Indeed, many Americans felt that we had paid very dearly for this material and believed the job could be done with it. But Wallace soon discovered that most of the equipment was hopeless. The jungle actually had eaten through the boilers of locomotives. Such buildings as the French had erected were rotting, and the sanitary conditions from one end of the proposed route to the other were very bad. A great amount of work would have to be done before the area could house and feed the army of workers. Nothing less than an army of workers could answer the demands of the Commission, the President, and the people of the United States to "make the dirt fly."

What Wallace had to do, in effect, was to take a strip of jungle and turn it into Main Street before he could hope to get down to building the canal. His first workers quit in droves. They learned that everything was three or four times as expensive as in the States. They had to buy drinking water in the dry season, live in what would have been a vile slum at home, and their stomachs rebelled at the food.

Wallace worked hard but he soon found that he did not have complete authority. As a railroad engineer he had had control of the purchase of necessary equipment and stores. Now he found himself tied down in the world of "orders in triplicate" and other red tape. As he feared, he had to await the rubber stamp of men seated 2,000 miles away from the immediate problems that faced him. Admiral John G. Walker, chairman of the Commission, had a vivid horror of the taint of graft, having studied at length the dreary experience of the French attempt to build a canal. He insisted on long and careful study of every request presented by Wallace, not because he doubted Wallace's honesty in any way but because he was a careful man by nature.

Urgent requests for equipment, cabled by Wallace to Washington, were studied for weeks and sometimes months by Admiral Walker and other members of the Commission. Often, to save money, bids for material went to firms with little or no experience. Thus, further delays resulted. Wallace himself was warned repeatedly not to send so many requests by cable, because of the cost. A ditch dug for an extensive drain-pipe system caved in and reverted to jungle while awaiting the arrival of the pipes.

At home there were charges that Wallace was wasting time and money. People could not understand why work was not moving forward. Dissatisfied ex-employees told gloomy tales to their hometown newspapers about conditions in general and the scourge of yellow fever in particular.

Wallace's spirits sank still further when President Theodore Roosevelt admitted that he had offered Elihu Root a salary of up to $100,000 a year to take complete charge of the canal building.

Then something else. The President dissolved the seven-man Commission and told Secretary of War William Howard Taft that he was especially displeased with Admiral Walker. Chief Engineer Wallace was left in office and made a member of the new Commission which Roosevelt appointed on April 1, 1905. Its chairman was another railroad man, Theodore P. Shonts. This event seemed to strengthen Wallace's hand.

Exhausted after a year's work in the Canal Zone, Wallace returned to the United States for a short vacation and to aid in the reorganization of the Commission. While at home, he was criticized for not doing his duty.

Wallace was losing his appetite for the job.

100

On his return to Panama he discovered that the new Commission was almost as difficult to work with as the old one. Its members were unhappy because some received larger salaries than others.

Wallace returned to New York, presumably to buy needed new equipment but actually to have a showdown with the highest authorities available. Perhaps to his surprise, his threat to resign succeeded only in angering Secretary Taft who, with the President's permission, accepted the resignation in a stinging public statement. Secretary Taft's words came as a shock to the average American, who had looked upon Wallace as a great public figure.

The job of Chief Engineer was then given to John F. Stevens, a close friend and admirer of Wallace. His was a more determined personality and he was promised the free hand that, somehow, had never been fully extended to Wallace. Chairman Shonts hailed this well-known railroad engineer as "a leader; a man who knows how to drive, what to expect from his subordinates, and how to enlist their enthusiasm and support."

Just before Stevens' departure for Panama, he was told by Roosevelt to go to him directly whenever he needed men or equipment or administrative changes—and to forget the authority of the War Department over Canal matters.

A considerable crowd of Canal workers met Stevens' ship when it docked at Colon. They had not assembled to welcome him. They were there to board the ship for the return voyage. The fear of disease hung over them, and they made no effort to hide their disgust over living conditions and the high price of food they had difficulty swallowing.

Stevens soon became aware of the great house-cleaning job that had confronted and beaten down Wallace. And he became aware of something more: the Canal would need

WALLACE, STEVENS, AND GORGAS

locks . . . locks that could lift traffic as high as eighty-five feet to get it over the mountains.

Stevens recognized, too, that the three greatest trouble makers in Panama were "yellow fever, malaria and cold feet—and the greatest of these is cold feet." To warm both feet and spirits he strongly backed the continuation of sanitary work, by that time regarded as a waste of money. In addition, he set up cold-storage lockers and a system of food shipments from the United States which in time enabled him to feed 17,000 men 2,000 miles from home.

To lift the hearts of those already on the job, and to make Canal work more attractive to men back home, Stevens provided recreation clubs and even formed a large orchestra. Its music in time resounded through the length and breadth of the Zone.

To move his equipment back and forth across the Isthmus, Stevens rebuilt the rotting old Panama Railroad and doubled its trackage. From

Washington he demanded (and got) equipment on a massive scale: a hundred of the biggest steam shovels ever made, 120 locomotives, 800 flatcars. He allowed no interference from small politicians and won the confidence of the rank and file among the workers in a number of ways. He refused to live in the rich quarters assigned to him and took up residence in a tin-roofed shack on the slope of Culebra Cut.

Dissatisfied men who brought their troubles to Stevens found him a fair judge. However, those who tried his patience too far were invited to step outside, roll up their sleeves, and do battle with him—with bare fists. No laborer on the Canal put in more hours than Stevens. When his steam-shovel men went on strike in 1906 he sent the lot of them back home. On the chance that Congress in time would approve a lock-type canal he retained Joseph Ripley, Lock Superintendent at Sault Ste. Marie . . . and kept digging.

Stevens' men and machines clawed 70,630 yards of earth and rock out of Culebra Cut in December, 1905, and stepped it up to 120,990 yards the following month, at a much smaller

cost. By June the monthly rate had risen to nearly a quarter of a million yards. Stevens, in a burst of fervor, suggested that his workers forget the eight-hour day clause in their agreements. If they refused he threatened that the Commission would dismiss them and bring in Chinese labor. He himself was averaging eighteen hours of work each day.

Perhaps Stevens' greatest feat during this period was his successful campaign for a lock Canal. It meant overcoming considerable and powerful opposition. A presidentially appointed board of consulting engineers which included engineers from France, Germany, England and Holland, reported to the Senate on May 17, 1906, that it favored a sea-level canal. Stevens argued gallantly against the verdict and won his first important champion in Taft, who had made two trips to the Zone and was familiar with the problems of a sea-level route.

Taft arranged for Stevens to present his case before Congressional committees on a number of occasions and, privately, wrote the speeches of senators who had come to his aid. He spread his charts and maps on the President's desk and pounding that desk with his emphatic fist, won Roosevelt to his side. As a result, the Board's decision was changed, and a lock-canal was decided upon.

Stevens, knowing now just what he had to do, announced at the end of 1906 that the Canal would be opened by January 1, 1915. His was a confidence that could move mountains, and it did.

Late in 1906 President Roosevelt went to Panama on the battleship *Louisiana* for a first-hand study of Stevens' progress—the first President to set foot on what amounted to a foreign land. What he saw pleased him and, being a strong, active man, he saw a lot. When the reception committee, including Stevens, arrived to welcome the President ashore at 7:30 one morning in November, Roosevelt walked down the pier from the shore side and announced that he had been rowed ashore two hours earlier and had toured Colon and the country around it on foot.

For the inspection tour that followed, the President made countless speeches from the observation platform of the train that took him across the Isthmus. He ate the food of the workers instead of that which had been planned for him, and healed the wounds of certain Panamanian officials with his speeches of friendship. He closed his whirlwind visit with a promise to decorate "those engaged in this war."

In his final speech he said:

"You are doing a work the like of which has not been seen in the ages, a work that shall last through the ages to come, and I pledge you as President of the United States, and speaking for the people of the United States, every ounce

110

of support and help and assistance that it is in my power to give you, so that we together, you backed by the people of the United States, may speedily bring this greatest of works to a triumphant conclusion."

He was especially pleased with the work of Stevens. Yet the chief engineer's days were numbered. He began to encounter a lot of the supervision from Washington that had hampered Wallace. Contracts were let to private firms which had little experience in such matters. When they failed, Stevens was blamed. The engineer began to be criticized at home by those who had failed to succeed under him. The printed criticism outweighed such achievements as moving 639,112 cubic yards out of Culebra in February, 1907, and 815,270 yards in March of that year.

Stevens believed that contracts involving the Canal should be let only to firms capable of supplying good men, good know-how and good equipment. Commissioner Shonts did not quite agree with Stevens. The Commissioner's views were strengthened by a statement that came from Secretary of War Taft. The Secretary said that some contractors weren't being given a fair chance to bid for canal work because of get-the-work-done demands.

Stevens and Shonts had worked very closely together in most matters. Now there was a somewhat unfriendly feeling between them. It was getting worse when Shonts abruptly quit to take a transportation job in New York City that paid him much more than he was getting with the Commission. Matters came to a head when Roosevelt and Taft gave an important contract to a firm which Stevens felt would do little except waste taxpayers' money. By cable, Stevens demanded an explanation from the President and from Taft. The cable annoyed both officials. The President did what he could to explain his action to the angry engineer, but

112

added, "I would not be willing now to alter this policy entered into with such deliberation . . ."

Stevens then resigned in a letter to the President. The letter stated that he would rather be Chief Engineer of the Canal project than President of the United States. However, he went on to say, he had become too discouraged by attacks from the rear by people "I would not wipe my boots on." Angrily, Roosevelt decided that Stevens must go at once.

And on this unpleasant note the second great civilian engineer left the Canal Zone, and once again there was dismay and bewilderment in the States. And maybe a knowing nod in France.

But in addition to their engineering contributions, Wallace and Stevens had taken an important step.

Each had supported the quietly impressive work of Colonel (later Major General) William

113

Crawford Gorgas, their chief Sanitary Officer. He served the Zone and fought its many diseases from 1904 until the first ship passed through the finished canal.

Gorgas and his patient assistants made it possible for workers other than Jamaicans and natives to live in the Canal Zone.

Men and women had been dying of nameless "fevers" on the Isthmus from the time the first Europeans attempted to cross it. The maladies first came to the attention of the United States early in 1850 when the pioneers of the Panama Railroad were at work. John C. Trautwine and many of his aides were laid low by something neither they nor their medical advisers could fathom.

Adolphe Godin de Lepinay, the ignored father of the lock-canal for the Isthmus, had written at length about the need of conquering the tropical diseases of the Isthmus if the French were to have a canal. He had been dismissed as a dreamer. De Lesseps succeeded for a time at least in turning his back, and that of the French company, on the obvious danger. But his men and their families continued to die. The old Frenchman clung steadfastly to an early boast, made on his first visit to Panama: "Only drunkards and the dissipated take the yellow fever and die."

The words "yellow fever" became a menace in the United States newspapers late in 1904, and they began to frighten men who might have applied for jobs on the Canal. Wallace and his wife, despite the coffins they had brought along with them, did their best to calm these fears in the Zone and the States by riding through the littered streets of boom towns along the Canal route, making light of the trouble.

But the death from yellow fever of Wallace's private secretary, at the very time Wallace was stumping in an effort to lessen the terror of the disease, had an alarming effect. It and later

115

deaths in the epidemic early in 1905 caused a great many workers to return to the United States. In May, 1905, there were thirty-three who became ill with the disease, and seven of these died. As the number of deaths increased, coffins of yellow-fever victims were hidden at railroad stations and docks before shipment back to the States.

There were sixty-two cases of yellow fever in June, 1905. Before the last case was reported on December 11 of the same year, the Americans had recorded 246 cases of the disease and eighty-four deaths.

There would have been many more deaths without Dr. Gorgas and his assistants—and without the aid given to them, sometimes against the wishes of the Commission, by Wallace and Stevens. At first Gorgas was called "that crank." People forgot that during and after the Spanish-American War he had done a fine job of fending off tropical diseases from American troops in Cuba. Now, in Panama, he went about his work as if he were deaf to the taunts. He insisted that huts and houses and barracks of workers be screened, that the smallest puddles be drained or treated with larvae-killing insecticides, and that every hovel be disinfected.

Gorgas feared malaria more than yellow fever. He preached sleeping under mosquito nets, the drinking of boiled water, and the avoidance of malaria carriers which he successfully identified. When his zeal for these preventives was frowned upon by the Commission, Gorgas found strong supporters in Wallace and then Stevens. The latter once saved Gorgas' job when Shonts attempted to put another man in his place.

Gorgas had to fight for many of the medical supplies sent to him from the States, and was constantly at odds with Panamanians who resented the fumes of the germ-killing drugs he shot through their homes. He brought religious wrath down on his head by fumigating a cathedral. But he stuck to his flit guns to the end, and died a well-rewarded and honored man in 1920.

CHAPTER VI

Goethals

THE SUDDEN RESIGNATION OF THEODORE ROOSE-velt himself would not have been more of a shock to the country than the resignation of Stevens. Except in certain quarters newspaper reports on Stevens had been enthusiastic. He was the Great Builder of his time; the man who would show the rest of the world, especially the French, that the United States could finish whatever it started. He was the symbol of America's growing might. Now, without warning, he was done.

Politically, it was a crisis for Roosevelt, who considered that the Panama Canal and its completion would rank in the pages of history with the Louisiana Purchase. He was determined that the Canal must suffer no further delays caused by the comings and goings of its Chief Engineers. Roosevelt thundered, "I propose now to put it in charge of men who will stay on the job till I get tired of having them there, or till I say they may abandon it. I shall turn it over to the United States Army."

It was odd that he should have used the word "abandon" for that was farthest from his thoughts.

As the man who would "stay on the job" he

122

chose a remarkable 49-year-old officer in the Army's Corps of Engineers, George Washington Goethals, a long-time friend and one-time informal aide-de-camp of Taft.

Goethals was already familiar with the problems involved. As a major he had accompanied Taft to the Canal Zone in 1905, on Taft's second trip. When Taft became enthusiastic over the progress that had been made in the previous twelve months, Goethals didn't quite agree. He thought the whole thing was hopeless and was not slow in saying so. He confided to Taft that he would have done certain things in a different manner. Taft did not forget. When Theodore Roosevelt asked his aid in the search for a man who would not be able to resign short of facing a court martial, Taft immediately thought of Goethals.

The call to Goethals from the White House arrived late at night, during a party. He put on his uniform and went immediately to see Roosevelt. Before the night was over the two men shook hands—and the Panama Canal had its final engineer.

Goethals came away from the White House burning with the same determination that the President felt. Roosevelt had given him what amounted to a blank check. If the Commission got in Goethals' way, as it could by both law and disposition, Goethals was to push it aside. As for Roosevelt, he would "assume powers which the law did not give," he told Goethals.

"The Canal must be built!" the President shouted, clenching his fists.

It was an order from the Commander-in-Chief of the armed forces to an officer.

It was not a popular appointment among the men in the Canal Zone. With an Army man at the top they felt they would be "drafted" and subjected to military justice and courts if things went wrong. Even some of those who had rebelled against the driving tactics of Stevens now

124

signed petitions asking either for him to recon-
sider his resignation or remain as their spokesman. When that failed they showered him with
gifts of a lasting nature.

Roosevelt, recognizing the importance of
good feeling among the workers, appointed
Stevens as chairman of the Commission shortly
before Goethals arrived at Cristobal in March,
1907—accompanied by two other fine Army Engineers, Majors D. D. Gaillard and W. L. Sibert.

There was one tense moment at the pier. A re-
porter loudly asked Goethals what changes he
intended to make. It was the big question on
everyone's mind, from the Commissioners down
to the humblest pick and shovel man.

"No changes whatsoever will be made in this
splendid organization," Goethals answered
evenly.

If Goethals had any doubts about the ability
of Stevens they soon disappeared as he and the
other Army men toured the Zone and inspected

the work. Goethals was astounded by the amount of work that had been done since his last trip. And his breath was taken away by the obstacles which had been overcome and those which still remained. But there had grown within him an admiration for Stevens which was later to find expression in such writings as:

> "The people talk about the success of the Army engineer at Panama, but it was fortunate that Mr. Stevens preceded us. The real problem of digging the Canal had been the disposal of the spoil and no Army engineer in America could have laid out the transportation scheme as Mr. Stevens did. We are building on the foundation he laid, and the world can not give him too much credit."

Goethals made a point of speaking to as many of the common workers as possible in or-

der to quiet their fears of "militarism." He praised their hero, Stevens, and in his great hearty voice laughingly told them that he didn't expect any of them to salute him. There would be no locks on the doors of his offices or his shacks, he told them. If they had a complaint, he wanted to hear it with his own ears.

Stevens remained in the Canal Zone just long enough to show one and all that he, too, felt that Goethals was the man to finish the job. When he was content that there was complete trust in the Army man, he resigned his post on the Commission and, with tears from some of his men, sailed for home.

Goethals was the lone boss of the works, for he inherited Stevens' job as chairman of the Commission, in addition to his labors as Chief Engineer. His authority was absolute. But he had not sought this power. In fact, when he first heard what the President had in mind he sent a note to the White House pointing out that laws concerning the Canal forbade one person's having so much authority.

Roosevelt replied that he didn't care about the laws, he wanted the Canal built.

Goethals needed all the authority he was given. To his surprise the steam-shovel men struck again and, when their terms weren't met, many left their jobs and returned to the United States. Goethals imported new crews in wholesale lots. His vast equipment orders were quickly approved in Washington. By the end of 1907 he had nearly 30,000 men at work, and excavation in Culebra Cut had reached (during December) the impressive figure of 1,025,485 cubic yards.

He was pestered now and then by visiting Congressmen. One group came from Capitol Hill, supposedly to check on the mounting costs of the operation, but actually there for a vacation. The members of the group complained that the workers were being paid too much and that their quarters were, in many cases, too comfortable! One of these Congressmen insisted on inspecting the upstairs of Goethals' own home, and the Colonel physically barred him.

It angered the Congressman. "I'm just wondering," he said to the hard-working Army man, "if, on my own salary of $7,500 a year, I would receive a place like this to live in if I worked here."

129

"Sir," Goethals answered coolly, "if *you* worked in the Canal Zone I don't think you would make $7,500 a year."

Goethals had Congress to combat and appeal to and satisfy for the next three years, but that task—which would have taken the full time of an average man—in no way interfered with the progress of the Canal. A greater distraction were his occasional quarrels with his Army associates, especially Major Sibert, over methods of dealing with the Canal's many problems. Goethals also had an occasional squabble with Gorgas's men, whose zeal to put larvae-killing oil on anything liquid caused them once to pour it on the still unset cement of the Gatun Locks and the Holy Water fonts of the Cathedral.

Goethals scoured the world for the best manpower, meanwhile making the Zone and its work more and more attractive to American workers. He set up bakeries and ice plants, completed more recreation clubs and hotels, and let the word spread back to the States—including the word that good cheap plank steaks were to be had almost everywhere. These were served on wooden platters carved from the old ties of the Panama Railroad.

The work finally took on a United Nations flavor, which the *Saturday Evening Post* in 1908 described in these terms:

> "The man who ran the steam shovel, who had charge of the engine and maneuvered it, was an Irishman. The man on the crane, who attended to the dumping, was an American. The two stokers at the engine behind were Jamaican Negroes, and the six members of the 'move up' crew, the men who leveled the ground where the shovel stood and placed the tracks so that it could move forward and keep its nose to the bank, were Sikhs from

the north of India, who wore white turbans on their heads and worked like automatons."

Harnessing the wild Chagres River, and using it to create Gatun Lake—the seventeen-and-a-half-mile long waterway which sits eighty-five feet up in the air like a muffler around the neck of the mountain range—was a tremendous effort.

It necessitated the building of a dam 8,400 feet long, 105 feet high, 2,200 feet thick at its base and a hundred feet across the top. In the course of its difficult construction Goethals had to answer a strange rumor. Someone started the tale that under the dam there was a hidden lake with a weak covering of earth above it, and that in time this would cave in, taking with it the earthworks dam and the expensive locks. This story gave those in favor of a sea-level Canal another field day in Congress and in the

134

American newspapers. Roosevelt, about to leave the White House, was forced once again to send Secretary of War Taft (the President-elect) to Panama for a first-hand inspection. Taft confirmed the strength of the dam, and the sea-level champions were put to rout again.

Work on the revised Gatun Locks, two sets of three each, was begun in August, 1909. This was followed a few months later by work on the intricate locks on the Pacific side: one lockage at Pedro Miguel, where shipping is brought down from the level of Gatun Lake to little Miraflores Lake, and then later down two vast lock-steps to the level of the Pacific. So well streamlined had the Goethals operation become by then that the officer let contracts for the manufacture of the incredible lock-gates. The specifications called for the last one of these to be safely on its hinges by January 1, 1914.

To keep the mountains of cement and steel and other material moving steadily to the lock sites, Goethals had to move the tracks of the Panama Railroad and its sidings almost constantly. The great worth of that railroad was exceeded only by the difficulties in changing its course and shape. During the peak years of the Canal's construction it would handle nearly 600 train movements a day.

But the job that held the fascination of the United States and the rest of the world was the job of digging through Culebra.

As the man-made valley became deeper, it cut the mountains in two. The adjoining cliffs it formed were given names which were to be known throughout the world: Gold Hill and Contractor's Hill. The digging called for the kind of teamwork which J. B. Bishop, the Canal historian, described as "a swarming mass of men and rushing railway trains, monster-like machines, all working with ceaseless activity, all animated seemingly by human intelligence, without confusion or conflict anywhere."

As many as fifty of the earth's largest steam-shovels clawed angrily at the uncertain rock and earth from seven each morning until five in the afternoon. Through the night, under garish lights, repair crews tended to the steam-shovels' needs so that they would be ready the following morning. In the rainy season, to protect the ugly but precious wound in the mountain from flash-floods, men worked 'round the clock building dams to keep water from stopping the work. By the late summer of 1909 Culebra had been cut down to forty feet above sea level at one point, and the debris was being moved out of the Cut at the rate of a million and a quarter cubic yards a month.

Though Goethals was, of course, in overall charge, two others were gaining fine reputations back in the United States for this particular part of the Canal job. They were Major Gaillard, in direct charge of the operation, and a brilliant Irish-American, L. K. Rourke. What the United States did not know was that, in time, the two men scarcely spoke to each other. To Goethals' disappointment Rourke quit in the spring of 1910 to become Superintendent of Streets in Boston.

The change in the Administration in Washington, with Taft going into the White House, fortunately had little effect on the Canal effort. Taft and Goethals had been friends for many years, and Taft's admiration for and support of the Army engineer increased during his visit to the Isthmus in November, 1910. The President returned to Washington to tell the nation that victory over enormous obstacles was in sight.

The next time Goethals appeared before Congressional appropriation committees, he was given a standing ovation.

Victory was, indeed, in sight.

CHAPTER VII

Victory

IN CONGRESS MEN WERE SERIOUSLY DEBATING
such questions as "Which type of ship shall be
the first to pass through the Panama Canal?"

In the Panama Canal Zone no one, especially Goethals, cared. Their task was to complete the gigantic machine—and the Panama Canal *is* a machine—so that any kind of ship could pass through it.

While Gatun Lake slowly rose against its man-made Dam of the same name, and against the shifty shoulder of the mountains, there were thousands of details to occupy Goethals' mind and talents.

There were problems, too. One of the fairly simple ones was that of moving angry Panamanians out of the way of the rising waters of Gatun Lake. Many climbed to the roofs of their little homes in the belief that the waters would subside. Among the more difficult problems was that of combating the tremendous landslides in Culebra Cut. These slides would wipe out backbreaking months or years of work and bury tens of thousands of dollars' worth of equipment.

In spite of all the problems, work went on. Concrete-pouring at the Miraflores Locks was completed May 17, 1913, and at the Gatun Locks two weeks later. In between those two dates—on May 20, to be exact—one of the great milestones in the creation of the Canal was reached.

Amidst ear-splitting explosions of dynamite and the scream of whistles, two steamshovels, advancing from opposite directions, met each other at the bottom level of Culebra Cut.

The imposing mountain that had dismayed men since the time of Columbus had been slashed in two!

On September 26 of that same year, Goethals walked up and down along a vantage point overlooking Gatun Locks. His hands were dug deeply into his pockets, and there was a great fear in his heart. The weather was stifling and sweat poured from him, but he did not notice. For this was the day for which he and countless others had labored. This was the day when the first of the locks would be tested.

At a signal from the great engineer, Gatun Lake was tapped. Its stored waters, now of considerable width and breadth, gushed into the brace of locks on high—nearest of the three groups to the Lake. Slowly, surely, the enormous doors of the two lower groups of locks opened to receive the overflow, and, in time, appeared like enormous swimming pools. The crowds along the banks of the locks laughed at the frogs which had come down from the Lake, obviously against their wills.

At precisely 4:45 p.m. on that historic September 26, 1913, a little tugboat named *Gatun* entered the lower lock. Behind it a mammoth steel gate closed, and a great hiss of water elevated it to the second lock . . . then to the third . . . and then onto Gatun Lake.

That much of an achievement behind them, Goethals and his men moved on to the milestone of letting diked water into Culebra Cut. The dike was laced with dynamite charges and, as befitted the occasion, a President of the United States was called upon to set them off.

He was President Woodrow Wilson, freshly come to office and as aware of the importance of the Panama Canal as had been earlier Presidents. At 2:00 p.m. on October 10, 1913, Wilson pressed a key on his desk in the White House. When the impulse reached the group of engineers, workers and champions of the Canal, waiting at a given spot near the entrance of the eight-mile gulch, there followed a terrific roar. The dike collapsed and a tidal wave of water plunged out of Gatun Lake into the greatest trench ever dug by man.

Among those present at the great hour were Philippe Bunau-Varilla, that questionable combination of French engineer and Panamanian statesman. He wept at what seemed the completion of his great dream.

The drama of the passage of the homely tugboat *Gatun* was reenacted on the Pacific side a few weeks later. Another tug, *Miraflores*, three barges and a launch were raised through the Miraflores Locks from the Pacific Ocean to Gatun Lake.

It was not until the end of that year that the waters of the Atlantic and Pacific were permitted to join in Culebra Cut, an event that made front-page news throughout the world and, subtly, changed the history of man.

The first complete passage through the canal was made by a humble crane boat, *Alexander La Valley*, January 7, 1914. This took place a month after the death in Baltimore, from a tumor of the brain, of the man who had done so much to whip the menace which had defeated the French—the cutting of the mountains. He was, of course, Colonel Gaillard.

Gaillard had been removed from the Canal Zone in the very early fall of 1913, completely exhausted by his labors. He died on December 5, 1913, and among those who deeply mourned him was the old associate with whom he had sometimes warred.

"Colonel Gaillard," wrote Colonel Goethals, "brought to the service trained ability of the first order, untiring zeal, and unswerving devotion to duty. His name is connected inseparably with the great task which was brought to completion under his guidance, and will be held in lasting honor."

A year and a half later President Wilson issued an executive order which, for all time, renamed the fabulous Culebra ditch "Gaillard Cut."

There were mountainous labors yet to be attended to. The military man in Goethals not only demanded of him that he leave the Canal in perfect condition to accept the shipping of the world. He also wanted to see to it that men by the thousands were trained to operate this vast and complex machine, and to protect it from any enemy who sought to throw a monkey-wrench into its intricate parts.

Costly slides, especially the so-called Cucaracha slide, had to be cleared. Additional scraping of the bottom of Gaillard Cut had to be attended to by dredges. Crews had to be taught to man the huge lock-gates. Pilots had to be schooled to guide the ships across the Isthmus. Interfering committees from Washington had to be controlled. The fighting side of the Army had to be held back in its efforts to build up within the Canal Zone a series of army bases which might anger the Panamanians. (Goethals laughed at the fears of the Signal Corps, then in charge of United States aviation, that there must be defenses against a possible enemy attack from the air.)

Goethals asked the United States and other nations to send ships to the Canal as guinea pigs

in the great experiment of training lock crews
and pilots. Many countries responded. From
both ocean sides ships were raised through

locks to Gatun Lake and returned to their respective oceans. "Know-how" was in the making.

As the day of the formal opening approached, Goethals arranged a dress rehearsal that would persuade even him that his work was done. On August 3, 1914, with the clouds of World War I heavy on the horizon, the sizable Panama Railroad ship *Cristobal* moved toward the Gatun Locks.

The *Cristobal* was given a clumsy crossing of the Isthmus but one which did no damage to the delicate locks.

Now came the great day of the formal opening of the Canal to commerce, on August 15, 1914. The first vessel was another ship from the fleet of the Panama Railroad, the *Ancon*, loaded with dignitaries ranging downward from President Belisario Porras of Panama. The *Ancon* came in early from the Atlantic side, was in Gatun Locks for an hour and a quarter, entered

Culebra Cut before noon of that day, and was sliding over the waters of the Pacific in mid-afternoon. Goethals, too nervous to be aboard, followed her through the route as best he could, watching the work of those handling the locks.

At the end of a nerve-wracking twenty-hour day Goethals flung himself into bed, like the exhausted warrior he was.

What he had done remains a subject that captivates not only the historian but the engineer. He had defeated the great strength of Nature, disease, pessimism, false optimism, politics, labor strife, and countless disorders.

He had finished a canal that goes up (actually south, because of the twist of the Isthmus) the valley of the Chagres on the Atlantic slope, passes through Gaillard Cut, and drops to the Pacific down the valley of the Rio Grande.

It was (and is) a canal which measures 40.27 statute miles in length from shore line to shore line, and 50.72 miles from deep water to deep water. The average ship can pass through the machinery of the Canal in about eight hours.

The terminus of Panama City on the Pacific shore actually is located about twenty miles east of Colon on the Atlantic side, because of the writhing of the Isthmus. The Canal itself runs from northwest to southeast.

The Atlantic sea-level section of the canal is just under seven miles, and about twenty-four miles of lake (Gatun) water lie between the uppermost Gatun Lock and Gaillard Cut. The Cut is eight miles long. After the drop-down through the Pacific side locks there are eight miles of sea-level route to the ocean.

The three steps of Gatun Locks cover a mile and a fifth. All of the Panama Canal Locks have a usable length of 1,000 feet, a width of 110 feet and hold about seventy feet of water.

Except for the cost of dredging out an especially bad slide which occurred on October 14,

1914 and closed the Canal for seven months, Goethals would have completed his job not only before the scheduled time but within his budget.

As it turned out the completed and workable Canal cost the United States $366,650,000. This does not include Army and Navy defenses and the payments to France and Panama. Of this sum thirty major slides used up $10,000,-000. A little under a quarter of a billion cubic yards of earth had been moved by the Americans.

On the night that Goethals flung himself into bed after the passage of the *Ancon,* he knew that while his own work was ninety-nine per cent complete the Canal itself would always be in a state of building. It was too big an undertaking ever to complete, really.

What he could not know was that from the beginning it would be profitable. The Canal has never had a losing year since the day the *Ancon*

153

passed through. This remains true although additional hundreds of millions of dollars have been poured into it, shoring up its slides, increasing its efficiency, manning its controls, oiling its gates. At last report it was earning a little better than two per cent on an investment of more than half a billion dollars.

Anyway, it is said, Goethals slept well that night of August 15, 1914, and his name has been revered ever since. And it always will be. For he brought immense fame to the United States at a time when the older nations of the world did not consider us among the major powers. Four hundred years after Columbus had looked yearningly at the barrier that blocked him from the Indies, Goethals smashed through it to the benefit of the world.

CHAPTER VIII

United States-Panama Relations

FOR MORE THAN FORTY YEARS THE UNITED STATES Government gave time, attention and money to the Republic of Panama. As a result, what had started out as a poor province of Colombia won its independence and was able to defeat the threat of tropical diseases. More important, Panama became third only to Argentina and Uruguay among the Latin American nations with the highest standards of living.

But America failed to give as much willing friendship to Panama as it gave engineering and sanitary aids. Almost from the start the United States did not regard the Panamanian worker as the equal of the worker from North America.

Because of Jim Crow laws, Panamanians were unable to get proper schooling, housing, wages and equal opportunities. These unjust laws also applied to people who were grouped into the "Panamanian" class by Zone officials—notably the large number of Jamaicans who did so much of the manual labor attending the digging of the Canal.

The color line was extended even to the American Negro who found work in the Canal Zone or visited there. When the Brooklyn National League baseball team appeared in the Canal Zone in the late 1940s during a Spring training tour, their Negro star "Jackie" Robinson was not permitted to eat with his teammates.

The bitter fruit of this prolonged intolerance—a white worker might make from twenty-five to three hundred percent more money than a colored person doing the same work—was the slow but sure rise of anti-American feeling. Communists quickly made the most of the tense atmosphere. In December, 1947, the Assembly of the Republic of Panama voted 51–0 against renewing American leases on war-time bases built on soil adjoining the American-controlled Canal Zone.

The United States State Department knew the storm was brewing, and did what it could to soften the blow. On September 12, 1946, it released the following Joint Statement by the States:

> "Mindful of the objectives of the 1936 Treaty of Friendship and Cooperation and of the Defense Sites Agreement of May 18, 1942, and conscious of recent improvements in weapons and methods of warfare, the Governments of Panama and of the United States have agreed to consult on the most effective means for assuring the defense of the Panama Canal.

159

Consistent with the aforementioned Agreement of 1942, the United States has already returned to Panama seventy-one defense sites and is preparing to return immediately twenty-seven more.

"It is the desire of both Governments to fulfill their joint responsibilities for the adequate protection of the Canal. The two Governments have reiterated their unqualified endorsement of the traditional friendship and sovereign respect existing between them and the vital role which the Panama Canal plays in the defense of this hemisphere."

But the anti-American feeling in Panama swung a harder verdict, and on February 20, 1948, the State Department ruefully announced the text of a note presented to Mario De Diego,

Panama's Minister for Foreign Affairs, by United States Ambassador Frank T. Hines:

"I have the honor to refer to my note . . . regarding the rejection by the National Assembly of Panama of the Defense Sites Agreement. . . . As Your Excellency is aware, that agreement assured the effective protection of the Canal and played an important part in bringing about the successful termination of hostilities. (Ed. Note: World War II.) Although my Government has maintained the position that it continued to be entitled, under the express terms of the 1942 Agreement, to the use of the defense sites until one year after the date on which the definitive treaty of peace which brings about the end of the present war shall have entered into ef-

161

fect, it has nevertheless taken the necessary measures to withdraw from those few remaining sites which had not already been returned to Panama under the provisions of the Agreement.

"Inasmuch as the evacuation of the defense sites has now been completed, I have the honor, under instructions from my Government, to inform Your Excellency that the Government of the United States of America now considers the Agreement terminated and no longer in effect."

An earlier State Department note, during the period of diplomatic sparring, had ended: "Failure to conclude an agreement will not, of course, affect the normal friendly relations between the two countries."

It remained for the Governor of the Panama

Canal to express the deep concern of the United States when the diplomatic breakdown helped to place the security of the Canal in jeopardy. His report, coming on the heels of the breakdown, read:

"The importance of the Panama Canal to the national defense was evidenced in World War II by the transit in the period 1941-1945 of over 5,300 combat vessels and about 8,500 other military craft consisting of cargo and troop vessels. One and one-half billion dollars has been estimated as the saving in shipping costs effected during the war by use of the Canal. Until military operations are conducted in a manner entirely different from that which can be foreseen, the Panama Canal will continue to be essential to the security of the United States.

163

"The service rendered by the Panama Canal in support of overseas military operations was possible only because the Canal was never attacked or damaged."

CHAPTER IX

As the Canal Is
...and Might Be

LENGTH FROM SHORE LINE TO SHORE LINE—40.27 miles.

Length from deep water to deep water—50.72 miles.

Course—The Canal runs south from its entrance in Limon Bay on the Atlantic side, through the Gatun Locks to a point in Gatun Lake a distance of eleven and a half miles from the Canal's mouth. It then turns east and follows thereafter a generally southeasterly direction to the Bay of Panama.

Locks—There are six sets of two. Each lock is a box-like space, 1,000 feet long by 110 feet wide, in which the water can be raised or lowered. The lock walls are 81 feet high on the Atlantic side, and slightly higher on the Pacific. To make the Gatun Locks, 2,068,000 cubic yards of cement were used; the Pacific Locks, 2,440,000.

At each end of the lock chambers are found "mitering gates." They consist of two massive leaves that are sixty-five feet wide and seven feet thick. These gates, ranging from 47 feet 4 inches high to 82 feet high, are pivoted on the lock walls.

Passage through a Lock—The vessel proceeds into the lock forebay under its own power or it is pulled by a tug. The vessel then comes to a full stop. It proceeds through the lock under the power and control of four electric locomotives, located on adjoining lock walls.

If the vessel is moving on to a higher level, water flows into the lock and lifts the ship until it is as high as the next lock. The gates of the first lock are then opened and the ship is pulled into that next compartment.

Gatun Dam—This dam contains 23,000,000 yards of earth, rock, cement and piles. It is anchored to a natural 110-foot-high hill. Its spillway is 1,200 feet long and 285 feet wide, and the lake it holds incorporates a hydro-electric power plant which uses 31,000,000 cubic feet of water each year. The Canal locks use 41,000,000 cubic feet of water through a year.

Madden Dam—Madden Dam was completed in 1935, thus bearing out the belief of several

French Company engineers that the Panama Canal would need an extra water supply to slake the great thirst of its locks. The water held by Madden Dam enabled the Canal to operate twenty-four hours a day and thus increases the number of passages and the Canal's income. The Dam is a little under 1,000 feet long and backs up 27,000,000,000 cubic feet of water which maintains the level of Gatun Lake during dry seasons. Madden Dam's hydro-electic power plants supply much of the power for the operation of the entire Canal project.

Pacific Side Dams—Several in number, these have created Miraflores Lake, a mile in length and fifty-four feet above sea level, as opposed to the eighty-five foot sea level of Gatun Lake.

Tides—The average tidal range on the Pacific side is twelve and a half feet, though there have been tides as high as twenty-one and a half feet. On the Atlantic side tidal ranges average less than one foot.

Sea-level Sections—The Atlantic sea-level section is six and two-thirds miles long, the Pacific sea-level section about eight miles.

System of Tolls—Tolls, or fees charged for passing through the Canal, do not depend on the nature of the cargo carried, but on how much the ship is able to earn. The lowest cost per ton has been seventeen and five-tenths cents on a cargo ship that was carrying a heavy load of iron ore. From this toll, the costs range upward. The average cost of tolls per ton of cargo during 1950 was about sixty-nine cents.

Tolls are levied on net tonnage, which represents the sum of the spaces inside the ship that can be devoted to the carriage of cargo and passengers.

Operation and Maintenance—A Governor is head of the organization known as The Panama Canal, an independent establishment within the Government. The Governor also is President of the Panama Railroad Company, a United States corporation. He is answerable to the President of the United States, through the Secretary of the Army.

Treaties Involving the Canal—Several treaties have been made concerning the Canal. These date back to the railroad treaty of 1849. The most important, and latest, is one signed by the United States and the Republic of Panama on March 2, 1936 and ratified by the United States on July 27, 1939. Among other things, the Treaty increases the annual payment to Panama from $250,000 to $430,000; explains what persons may reside within the Canal Zone, and establishes certain rules about the conduct of trade and business.

Deficiencies of the Present Canal—The Canal offers several difficulties to ships that attempt to pass through it. Gaillard Cut is the most difficult section of the Canal to navigate, and it has

172

been necessary to limit traffic to one direction at night for all ships, and at all times for large or unwieldy vessels.

The present locks, 110 feet wide and 1,000 feet long, are not large enough to permit transit of aircraft carriers of the Midway class or of ocean liners like the*Queen Mary* and *Queen Elizabeth*.

The present locks must be overhauled every other year, and though the overhaul work is staggered, delays result none the less.

Third String of Locks Project—This was authorized in 1939, and the size of the proposed locks was increased to 200 feet by 1,500 feet a short time later. The cost was to be about three times that of the complete Panama Canal itself—or $1,143,000,000, to be exact. Work on the third locks was halted in May, 1942 because of the war and the realization that they would be as open to enemy attack as the old locks.

173

Present Canal

GATUN LOCKS

ATLANTIC

Proposed Canal

ATLANTIC

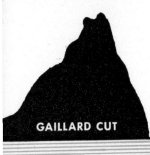

GAILLARD CUT   PEDRO MIGUEL
                   LOCKS.
                          MIRAFLORES LOCKS

                                PACIFIC

TIDAL LOCK   PACIFIC

Nine years later the work had not yet been resumed.

Annual Report of Governor of Panama Canal (1947)—In 1947, it was suggested that the Canal be rebuilt for two reasons:

1. To permit the passage of greater traffic, and the larger vessels expected in the year 2000;

2. To make the Canal as safe as possible from enemy attack.

At a cost of $2,308,000,000, the channel would be deepened and widened. The lock chambers would be increased in size to 150 feet by 200 feet.

The locks at Gatun and Miraflores would be built a great distance apart, so that in case of attack, they would not both be destroyed at the same time. Spare lock gates would be built for use while damaged gates were under repair.

The report ended, "Such a lock canal, while

176

providing the maximum security feasible in a lock-type canal, would not meet the future needs of national defense."

For this reason, perhaps, no action was taken on the plans.

In his report to President Truman in 1947 Governor Mehaffey recommended a sea-level route, a straight passage, which would cost approximately $2,500,000,000 and require 37,-000 workers for ten years. Under the plan, approved after years of study by Canal experts, more than 1,000,000,000 cubic yards of earth and rock would be excavated. Such a canal would be about five miles shorter than the present one and save about four hours in transit time. It was felt at the time of the proposal that "conversion could be accomplished without significant interference with the operation of the present Canal except for a period of approximately one week while Gatun Lake was being

177

drained and the water surface lowered to sea level."

No man can foretell the future of Columbus's "narrow land between two seas." But this much is certain: The great divisions of men and machinery necessary to create a newer, wider, deeper ditch across Panama will face a task greater than any in the history of engineering. Yet it will have been simplified for them.

It will have been simplified for them not so much by modern earth-moving and dredging equipment as by the human contributions of men now long since gone on to their reward . . . dreamers who ranged down the generations from Columbus to Theodore Roosevelt . . . and doers as different in time and temperament as Pedrarias, whose slaves built the first Isthmian path, to Goethals, whose associates managed, after the failure of the French, to deepen that path into a waterway short-cut through which nations and men may know one another better than before.

LANDMARK BOOKS

★